Missouri

BY ANN HEINRICHS

Content Adviser: Lynn Wolf Gentzler, Associate Director, The State Historical Society of Missouri, Columbia, Missouri

Reading Adviser: Dr. Linda D. Labbo, Department of Reading Education, College of Education, The University of Georgia

COMPASS POINT BOOKS ◆ MINNEAPOLIS, MINNESOTA

Compass Point Books
3109 West 50th Street, #115
Minneapolis, MN 55410

Visit Compass Point Books on the Internet at *www.compasspointbooks.com*
or e-mail your request to *custserv@compasspointbooks.com*

On the cover: The Gateway Arch and the Saint Louis skyline

Photographs ©: Dave H. Houser/Corbis, cover, 1; John Elk III, 3, 10, 28, 29, 35, 36, 37, 38, 40, 41, 42, 45, 47, 48 (top); Kent & Donna Dannen, 5, 8; Jim Wark, 6; Unicorn Stock Photos/James L. Fly, 9; Courtesy Missouri Department of Natural Resources/Missouri Resource Magazine, 11; Michael S. Lewis/Corbis, 12; Historical Picture Archive/Corbis, 13; Bettmann/Corbis, 14, 32; Hulton/Archive by Getty Images, 15; Corbis, 16, 17, 18; Museum of Flight/Corbis, 19; Greg Gorel/Visuals Unlimited, 20; Patrice Ceisel/Visuals Unlimited, 21; Unicorn Stock Photos/Martha McBride, 22; David Falconer, 24, 43 (top); AFP/Corbis, 25, 33; George Hall/Corbis, 26; Richard Thom/Visuals Unlimited, 27; Lynn Goldsmith/Corbis, 30; Courtesy Kansas City St. Patrick's Day Parade Committee/photograph by Patti Aylward-Kalb, 31; Robesus, Inc., 43 (state flag); One Mile Up, Inc., 43 (state seal); Unicorn Stock Photos/Bernard Hehl, 44 (top); Unicorn Stock Photos/Robert Vankirk, 44 (middle); PhotoDisc, 44 (bottom); Courtesy George Washington Carver National Monument, 46.

Editors: E. Russell Primm, Emily J. Dolbear, and Catherine Neitge
Photo Researcher: Svetlana Zhurkina
Photo Selector: Linda S. Koutris
Designer: The Design Lab
Cartographer: XNR Productions, Inc.

Library of Congress Cataloging-in-Publication Data
Heinrichs, Ann.
    Missouri / by Ann Heinrichs.
       p. cm. — (This land is your land)
    Summary: Introduces the geography, history, government, people, culture, and attractions of Missouri. Includes bibliographical references and index.
    ISBN 0-7565-0329-9
    1. Missouri—Juvenile literature. [1. Missouri.] I. Title. II. Series: Heinrichs, Ann. This land is your land.
    F466.3 .H45 2003
    977.8—dc21   2002010091

Table of Contents

NOTE: In this book, words that are defined in the glossary are in **bold** the first time they appear in the text.

Willard Vandiver was a U.S. congressman from Missouri. One night in 1899, he attended a dinner. There he spoke up.

"I come from a state that raises corn and cotton and **cockleburs** and Democrats," he declared. "Frothy eloquence [fancy talk] neither convinces nor satisfies me. I am from Missouri. You have got to *show me!*"

Ever since then, Missouri has been called the Show Me State. At least, that's what legends say. Missourians *are* very down-to-earth. They find it's useful to say, "Show me!"

Missouri sits just west of the Mississippi River. It was the gateway to the American West. Many westward-bound pioneers started out from or passed through Missouri. Missouri was also a crossroads for river traffic. The Mississippi and Missouri rivers come together there.

People of many **cultures** came together in Missouri, too. They brought their foods, festivals, and music.

Today, millions of visitors enjoy Missouri's mountains and lakes. The Show Me State shows them all a great time!

▲ The wide Mississippi River forms the eastern border of Missouri.

Mountains, Rivers, and Plains

▲ The Mississippi and Missouri Rivers meet near Saint Louis.

Missouri is a "neighborly" state. It has eight other states as neighbors. Iowa is north of Missouri. Arkansas is to the south. To the east are Illinois, Kentucky, and Tennessee. To the west are Nebraska, Kansas, and Oklahoma. Only Tennessee shares borders with that many states.

Missouri is a north central state. Sometimes it's called a Midwestern state. It lies between the Atlantic Ocean and the Rocky Mountains.

Two mighty rivers helped open up Missouri. One is the

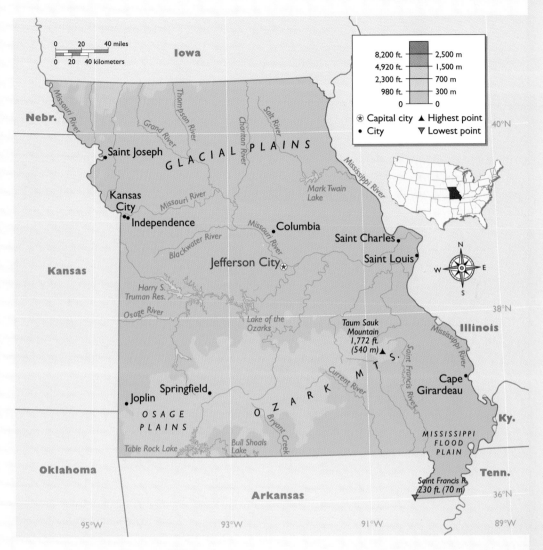

8,200 ft. — 2,500 m
4,920 ft. — 1,500 m
2,300 ft. — 700 m
980 ft. — 300 m
0 — 0

⊛ Capital city ▲ Highest point
• City ▼ Lowest point

Iowa

Nebr.

Missouri River

GLACIAL PLAINS

Thompson River

Grand River

Chariton River

Salt River

Mississippi River

40°N

Saint Joseph

Kansas City

Missouri River

Mark Twain Lake

Independence

Columbia

Missouri River

Saint Charles

Saint Louis

Blackwater River

Kansas

Jefferson City ⊛

Harry S. Truman Res.

Osage River

Lake of the Ozarks

38°N

Taum Sauk Mountain
1,772 ft.
(540 m) ▲

Illinois

Saint Francis River

Mississippi River

Joplin

Springfield

O S A G E
P L A I N S

O Z A R K   M T S.

Current River

Cape Girardeau

Bryant Creek

Ky.

Table Rock Lake

Bull Shoals Lake

MISSISSIPPI
FLOOD
PLAIN

Oklahoma

Tenn.

Saint Francis R.
230 ft. (70 m)
▼

36°N

Arkansas

95°W   93°W   91°W   89°W

▲ **A topographic map of Missouri**

Mississippi, the nation's longest river. It runs along
Missouri's eastern border. The other is the Missouri River.
It flows into the Mississippi near Saint Louis. Many other
rivers empty into the Mississippi and Missouri.

▲ Bagnell Dam is located on Lake of the Ozarks, one of Missouri's many human-made lakes.

Missouri's biggest lakes were formed by humans. People built dams on rivers to create these lakes. The largest are Lake of the Ozarks and Harry S. Truman Reservoir.

Northern Missouri is the Glacial Plains region. Huge **glaciers,** or ice sheets, once covered it. The glaciers smoothed the land into rolling plains. They also left rich soil that's great for farming. The Osage Plains cover southwest Missouri. They are fairly flat. Tall prairie grasses once waved across these plains.

▲ The plains of northern Missouri provide rich farmland.

▲ The Ozark Mountains are dotted with many lakes.

The Ozark Mountains stretch across southern Missouri. Thick forests cover these rugged hills. Swift rivers rush through their deep valleys. Many caves, lakes, and springs are scattered through the region.

Southeastern Missouri is called the Southeastern Lowlands. High **levees,** or walls, stand along the shore. They keep the Mississippi River from flooding the land. One town in this region is New Madrid (pronounced MAD-rid). It sits atop a **fault,** or crack in Earth's crust. This fault is the center of many powerful earthquakes.

Missouri's southeast corner sticks down like a boot heel. A farmer named John Hardeman Walker once lived there. He begged for his land to belong to Missouri. When Missouri became a state, Walker got his wish.

▲ **John Hardeman Walker was one of the farmers eager to have his land in the boot heel region become part of the new state of Missouri.**

▲ Deer roam across much of Missouri.

Forests cover much of Missouri. They're especially thick in the Ozarks. There you'll find opossums, chipmunks, raccoons, foxes, and deer. Quails and whippoorwills rustle around on the ground. Overhead are blue jays, cardinals, mockingbirds, and woodpeckers. Trout, bass, and catfish swim in the lakes and streams.

Northern Missouri has very cold winters. Chilly winds whip across the plains. The northwest gets the most snowfall. Southeastern Missouri has really hot summers.

A Trip Through Time

People called Mound Builders once lived in Missouri. Some of their huge mounds of earth still stand. Later, Sauk and Fox people settled the northern woodlands. They hunted wild game and fished in the streams. Missouri people lived along the Missouri River. They were to give their name to the whole state.

In the south and west were the Osage. They lived in farming villages and hunted buffalo. The Osage told the story of creation in long poems. They recited this story to each newborn baby.

French explorers were the first white people in Missouri. Jacques Marquette

▲ **The Missouri people gave their name to the state.**

▲ Jolliet (left) and Marquette explored the Mississippi River in Missouri with the help of Native American guides.

and Louis Jolliet arrived in 1673. Next came René-Robert Cavelier, Sieur de La Salle. In 1682, he claimed a vast region for France. It covered all lands whose rivers flow into the Mississippi. Of course, that included Missouri. La Salle named the region Louisiana, after France's King Louis XIV.

Soon more Frenchmen moved in. Missionaries opened Saint Francis Xavier mission near present-day Saint Louis in 1700. Miners and hunters founded Sainte Genevieve around

1750. The settlement still exists.

In 1803, France sold Louisiana to the United States. This Louisiana Purchase doubled the country's size! Meriwether Lewis and William Clark explored these new lands. They headed west on the Missouri River in 1804.

Missouri Territory was organized in 1812. Statehood, however, would be a problem. Southern states allowed slavery, while Northern states did not. Congress tried to keep a balance between the two sides.

▲ A mission named after Saint Francis Xavier was founded in 1700.

▲ The Santa Fe Trail connected Franklin, Missouri, to Santa Fe, New Mexico.

Finally, Congress agreed on the Missouri **Compromise.**
Missouri would have slavery, while Maine would not. Both
states joined the Union in 1821. That same year, the Santa
Fe Trail opened. It led from Franklin, Missouri, to what is
now Santa Fe, New Mexico. The Oregon Trail began in
Independence. Pioneers followed it to the northwestern
United States.

The slavery problem kept growing. Southern states began to secede, or leave the Union. Some Missourians wanted to secede, too. Missouri stayed in the Union after all. The fight over slavery led to the Civil War (1861–1865).

Missouri had grown quickly since statehood. **Immigrants** arrived from Germany, Ireland, and other countries. People from Southern and Midwestern states moved in, too. Saint Louis and Kansas City became centers for railroad shipping.

▲ A Civil War battle at Belmont, Missouri

▲ **A steel manufacturing plant in Saint Louis in 1918**

Other states shipped cattle to these cities, especially Kansas City. Farmers were shipping out tobacco and pork. Miners were digging out lead, coal, and zinc. New factories were making iron products.

In the 1930s, Missouri, like the rest of the United States, experienced the effects of the Great Depression. This was a time when many businesses failed and millions of Americans were out of work and homeless. It wasn't until World War II

(1939–1945) that Missouri, along with the rest of the country, began to recover. Missouri's mines and factories supplied aircraft for the war effort. After the war, new factories made cars, chemicals, and foods. More and more farmers took city factory jobs.

Manufacturing continued to grow. Tourism, however, was growing even faster. Today, visitors flock to Missouri by the millions. They enjoy its many historic sites and recreation areas.

▲ **Missouri was able to recover from the Great Depression partly because of the demand for aircraft production during World War II.**

Government by the People

Even children can take part in their government. Missouri school students proved it! Fourth graders in Stockton wanted the Eastern black walnut to be the state tree nut. So they

▲ **The Eastern black walnut**

▲ Missouri's state aquatic animal, the paddlefish

wrote letters to their state lawmakers. It worked! Lawmakers approved the new state symbol in 1990.

Students in other cities tried the same thing. Their efforts resulted in three new state symbols. The crinoid became the state fossil, the paddlefish became the state aquatic animal, and the channel catfish became the state fish.

▲ The state capitol in Jefferson City

Missouri's government is much like the U.S. government. It is divided into three branches—legislative, executive, and judicial. The legislative branch makes the state laws. Voters choose their lawmakers to serve in Missouri's general assembly. It has two houses, or parts. One is the 34-member senate. The other is the 163-member house of representatives.

▲ **A geopolitical map of Missouri**

The executive branch makes sure people obey the state's laws. Missouri's governor heads the executive branch. Missourians vote to choose a governor every four years. A governor can serve only two terms in a row. Many other officers help with executive jobs. Some are elected, while the governor appoints others.

The judicial branch is made up of judges. They decide whether a law has been broken. Missouri's highest court is the state supreme court.

▲ A statue of President Harry S. Truman stands in front of the Jackson County Courthouse in Independence.

Missouri is divided into 114 counties and the city of Saint Louis. Voters elect county commissioners and other county officers. Most cities elect a mayor and a city council.

Missourians are proud of their homegrown leaders. During World War I (1914–1918), Missourian John J. Pershing commanded the American Expeditionary Forces. General Omar Bradley was a great commander in World War II. Harry Truman was president of the United States. He served from 1945 to 1953. Richard Gephardt is a leader in the U. S. House of Representatives.

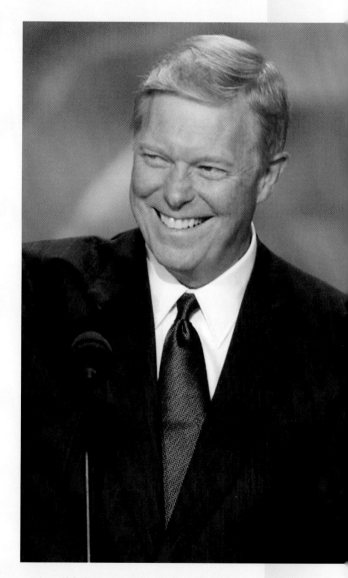

▲ **U.S. Representative Richard Gephardt**

Missouri makes things that *go!* Its factories make airplanes, cars, trucks, buses, and railroad cars. Transportation equipment is Missouri's major factory product. Chemicals are next in value. They include fertilizer, bug poisons, paint, soap, and medicines.

Many of Missouri's crops end up in factories, too. They become foods such as ice cream and flour. Saint Louis and Kansas City are the leading factory centers.

▲ **Production inside a Missouri airplane factory**

Travel through Missouri and you'll see miles of rolling farmland. Missouri is one of the nation's top farming states. It has more farms than any state except California. It's also a leader in many farm products. Missouri is the nation's second-highest producer of beef cattle. It ranks third in hay and sixth in soybeans and rice.

Beef cattle bring in the most farm income. Hogs, chickens, and turkeys are valuable farm animals, too. Soybeans,

▲ Cattle are an important Missouri farm product.

▲ **Missouri apples after the harvest**

corn, cotton, and hay are the top crops. Missouri farmers also raise apples, peaches, vegetables, and flowers.

Some of Missouri's earliest settlers were lead miners. Today, Missouri is the nation's top producer of lead. Limestone is another important mineral. It's crushed to make cement and build roads. Coal, clay, and iron are mined in Missouri, too.

Most Missouri workers hold service jobs. It's hard to imagine life without them! They work in schools, hospitals, stores, banks, and restaurants. Some work with sports teams. Others sell cars, fix televisions, or drive buses. They all use their skills to help others.

In 2000, there were 5,595,211 people in Missouri. That made it seventeenth in population among the states. Kansas City is Missouri's largest city. Next in size are Saint Louis, Springfield, and Independence.

Missourians' **ancestors** came from all over the world. Some came from Germany, Ireland, or England. Others were French, Italian, or Asian. About one out of every nine residents is African-American. All these people give Missouri a rich **heritage.**

▲ **Kansas City is known for its many fountains.**

Kansas City was a hot spot for jazz in the 1930s. Jazz clubs along 18th Street were jumpin' every night! Saint Louis was the place for ragtime and blues. Scott Joplin, called the King of Ragtime, lived there. So did guitarist Chuck Berry. His blues style gave birth to rock and roll. Both cities still have lively music clubs.

Many German immigrants settled in Hermann. The town holds a German festival in May and October. French culture is alive in Sainte Genevieve. It has a French festival every July

▲ **Guitarist Chuck Berry**

and August. Irish culture has its day in Kansas City on March 17, Saint Patrick's Day. A huge parade marches through town.

▲ The Saint Patrick's Day Parade in Kansas City

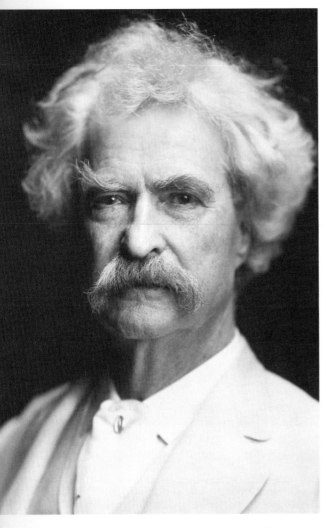

▲ Famous author and Missouri native Mark Twain

Author Mark Twain grew up in Hannibal. One of his best-loved tales is *The Adventures of Tom Sawyer.* Now Hannibal holds Tom Sawyer Days every July. Kids compete in Tom's least-favorite activity— painting fences!

Many other famous people called Missouri home. Author Laura Ingalls Wilder lived in Mansfield. There she wrote the Little House series of books. Actors Vincent Price and Jean Harlow were Missourians. So are John Goodman and Dick Van Dyke.

Did you ever hear the saying "It ain't over 'till it's over"? Baseball star Yogi Berra said it. He played for the New York

Yankees. Missourians, however, know he came from Saint Louis.

Missouri sports fans have plenty to cheer about. The Saint Louis Cardinals have won baseball's World Series nine times! In the 1985 World Series, Missourians couldn't lose. Their Kansas City Royals team played the Cardinals—and won. Missouri has two star football teams, too. The Saint Louis Rams won the 2000 Super Bowl. The Kansas City Chiefs won it in 1970.

▲ The Saint Louis Rams celebrate a touchdown during the 2000 Super Bowl.

As a boy, Mark Twain found a great hideout. It was a cave near Hannibal. Later that cave showed up in *The Adventures of Tom Sawyer*. Tom and his friend Becky got lost in it. You can explore Mark Twain's Cave, too. You can also tour Twain's boyhood home.

Speaking of caves, check out Meramec Caverns. It's a massive chain of awesome caves. Runaway slaves once hid there while escaping to freedom. The outlaw Jesse James hid there, too. Jesse's home in Saint Joseph is now a museum.

Saint Joseph is also known for the Pony Express. This mail service ran from 1860 to 1861. Riders galloped between Saint Joseph and Sacramento, California. Delivery time was ten days. That was fast for the 1860s! You'll get the whole story at the Pony Express Museum.

How did Missouri's pioneers live? See for yourself at Missouri Town 1855 in Lees Summit. You'll visit the village school, blacksmith shop, and stagecoach stop. Guides in

▲ **Meramec Caverns was once a popular hideout for runaway slaves and outlaws.**

▲ Fort Osage is in Sibley, which is northeast of Kansas City.

1800s clothing explain what's going on. Nearby Fort Osage offers another peek into the past. It was once the nation's westernmost fort. Now cooks, hunters, and farmers bring those days to life.

▲ The jazz district in Kansas City celebrates the many contributions African-Americans made to the country's musical heritage.

Kansas City is rich in African-American history. Its jazz district has two museums under one roof. One is the Negro Leagues Baseball Museum. It highlights black baseball

▲ **Harry S. Truman's former home in Independence**

players before the game was **integrated.** The American Jazz Museum honors 1930s jazz stars.

President Truman's library and museum are in nearby Independence. One exhibit is a model of his White House office. Truman's birthplace is farther south in Lamar.

Jefferson City is the state capital. It's right in the center of the state. In the capitol, you can watch state lawmakers in action. You won't travel far to the State Museum. It's on the first floor!

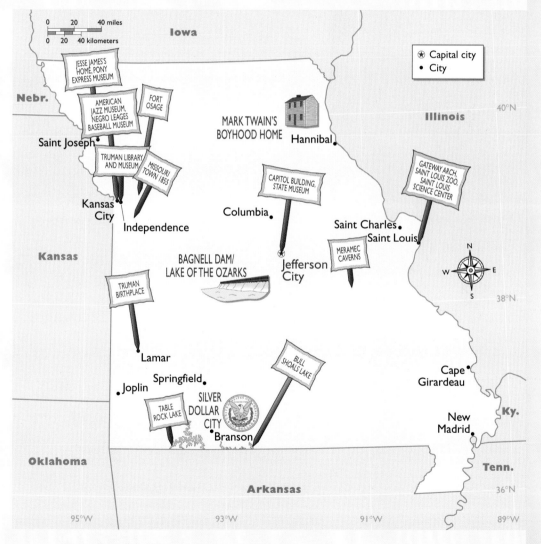

Places to visit in Missouri

▲ **The Gateway Arch rises behind Saint Louis's Old Courthouse, which has restored courtrooms and a museum.**

You know when you're near Saint Louis. You see its Gateway Arch from miles away. It honors Saint Louis as the gateway to the West. Once you're in town, check out the zoo. Six thousand animals prowl, slither, and hop around there. Then stop by the Saint Louis Science Center. This huge museum is full of hands-on science exhibits.

Many visitors find all they want in the Ozarks. Millions of people visit Branson every year. There they can see dozens of country music shows. Nearby is Silver Dollar City. It's built like an old mining town. Workers demonstrate log-cabin building and other crafts. Some visitors spend days at Lake of the Ozarks. Others like Table Rock or Bull Shoals lakes. They go boating or swimming. Many people like to hike through forests full of wildlife. They all agree—Missouri is a great place to explore!

Important Dates

1673 Jacques Marquette and Louis Jolliet pass the mouth of the Missouri River on their way down the Mississippi River.

1682 René-Robert Cavelier, Sieur de La Salle, claims the Mississippi River Valley for France. This area, which includes Missouri, is called Louisiana.

c.1750 Sainte Genevieve becomes Missouri's first permanent white settlement.

1764 Saint Louis is founded.

1803 Missouri passes to the United States in the Louisiana Purchase.

1804 The Lewis and Clark Expedition sets out from Saint Louis.

1812 Missouri Territory is established.

1821 Missouri becomes the twenty-fourth state on August 10.

1826 Jefferson City becomes the state capital.

1854–1856 People on the Missouri–Kansas border fight over the spread of slavery into Kansas.

1861–1865 Civil War battles take place in Missouri.

1904 Saint Louis hosts a World's Fair for the 100th anniversary of the Louisiana Purchase. The fair includes the first Olympic Games ever held in the United States.

1931 Bagnell Dam on the Osage River forms Lake of the Ozarks.

1945 Harry S. Truman of Independence becomes president of the United States.

1965 The Gateway Arch in Saint Louis is completed.

1993 The Missouri and Mississippi Rivers overflow, creating serious floods.

2000 Governor Mel Carnahan is elected to the U.S. Senate after he is killed in a plane crash. His wife Jean is appointed to take his place in the Senate.

Glossary

ancestors—a person's grandparents, great-grandparents, and so on

cockleburs—plants that shed prickly little balls

compromise—an agreement in which both sides give in a little

cultures—groups of people who share beliefs, customs, and a way of life

fault—a crack in Earth's crust

glaciers—huge sheets of ice

heritage—things of value that are passed down to later people

immigrants—people who come to another country to live

integrated—accepting of all races

levees—walls that keep water from flooding the land

Did You Know?

★ Ice cream cones were introduced at the Saint Louis World's Fair in 1904. An ice cream vendor at the fair ran out of paper cups. He asked the waffle vendor at the next booth to help. The waffle man rolled up waffles to hold the ice cream.

★ Saint Louis University is the oldest university west of the Mississippi River. It received its charter in 1832.

★ The nation's most powerful earthquakes struck in 1811 and 1812. Their center was New Madrid, Missouri. New Madrid sits on a break in Earth's crust called the New Madrid Fault.

★ Missouri was named after the Missouri group of Native Americans. Their name means "town of the large canoes."

★ Every spring, schools in Nixa close for Sucker Days. That's when people come from miles around for a fish fry. What do they fry? Local sucker fish!

★ Saint Louis's Gateway Arch is the tallest monument built in the United States. It stands 630 feet (192 meters) high.

★ It's said that Kansas City has more fountains than any city in the world except Rome, Italy.

State capital: Jefferson City

State motto: *Salus Populi Suprema Lex Esto* (Latin for, "Let the Welfare of the People Be the Supreme Law")

State nickname: Show Me State

Statehood: August 10, 1821; twenty-fourth state

Area: 69,709 square miles (180,546 sq km); **rank:** nineteenth

Highest point: Taum Sauk Mountain, 1,772 feet (540 m) above sea level

Lowest point: 230 feet (70 m) above sea level by the Saint Francis River near Cardwell

Highest recorded temperature: 118°F (48°C) at Clinton on July 15, 1936, at Lamar on July 18, 1936, and at Union and Warsaw on July 14, 1954

Lowest recorded temperature: −40°F (−40°C) at Warsaw on February 13, 1905

Average January temperature: 30°F (−1°C)

Average July temperature: 78°F (26°C)

Population in 2000: 5,595,211; **rank:** seventeenth

Largest cities in 2000: Kansas City (441,545), Saint Louis (348,189), Springfield (151,580), Independence (113,288)

Factory products: Transportation equipment, electrical equipment, food products

Farm products: Soybeans, beef cattle, corn, hogs, hay

Mining products: Lead, limestone, coal

State flag: Missouri's state flag has three wide stripes—red, white, and blue. In the center is the Missouri coat of arms. It features the same symbols as the state seal. Around it is a blue band with twenty-four stars. They stand for Missouri's place as the twenty-fourth state.

State seal: Two grizzly bears stand on each side of the state seal. They stand for Missourians' strength and bravery. The bears hold a round shield. The right half of the shield shows the coat of arms of the United States. The left half of the shield has a silver crescent moon and a grizzly bear.

Around the shield is the motto "United We Stand, Divided We Fall." Beneath the bears' feet is the state motto. At the top are one large star and twenty-three small stars. They stand for Missouri's place as the twenty-fourth state.

State abbreviations: Mo. (traditional); MO (postal)

State Symbols

State bird: Bluebird

State floral emblem: White hawthorn blossom

State tree: Flowering dogwood

State tree nut: Eastern black walnut

State animal: Missouri mule

State fish: Channel catfish

State aquatic animal: Paddlefish

State insect: Honeybee

State mineral: Galena

State rock: Mozarkite

State fossil: Crinoid

State musical instrument: Fiddle

State American folk dance: Square dance

Making Walnut Mini-Pies

Walnuts are Missouri's state nut.

Makes twenty-four mini-pies.

INGREDIENTS:

1 8-ounce package cream cheese

1/2 cup margarine, softened

1 cup flour

1 cup walnut pieces

2 eggs, beaten

1 cup brown sugar

1 teaspoon vanilla

1 tablespoon margarine

DIRECTIONS:

Make sure an adult helps with the hot stove! Preheat oven to 325°F. Blend cream cheese and 1/2 cup margarine, then mix in the flour. Chill for one hour. Divide dough into twenty-four sections. Place each section in the cup of a muffin tin. Press the dough to fit the shape of the cup. Sprinkle some walnuts on the dough. Mix eggs, sugar, vanilla, and 1 tablespoon margarine. Spoon a rounded tablespoon of this mixture into each muffin cup. Sprinkle the rest of the walnuts on top. Bake until dough is golden brown, about 20 to 25 minutes.

"Missouri Waltz"

Words by James R. Shannon, music by John V. Eppel

Hush-a-bye, ma baby, slumbertime is comin' soon;
Rest yo' head upon my breast while Mommy hums a tune;
The sandman is callin' where shadows are fallin',
While the soft breezes sigh as in days long gone by.

Way down in Missouri where I heard this melody,
When I was a little child upon my Mommy's knee;
The old folks were hummin'; their banjos were strummin';
So sweet and low.

Strum, strum, strum, strum, strum,
Seems I hear those banjos playin' once again,
Hum, hum, hum, hum, hum,
That same old plaintive strain.

Hear that mournful melody,
It just haunts you the whole day long,
And you wander in dreams back to Dixie, it seems,
When you hear that old time song.

Hush-a-bye ma baby, go to sleep on Mommy's knee,
Journey back to Dixieland in dreams again with me;
It seems like your Mommy is there once again,
And the old folks were strummin' that same old refrain.

Way down in Missouri where I learned this lullaby,
When the stars were blinkin' and the moon was climbin' high,
Seems I hear voices low, as in days long ago,
Singin' hush-a-bye.

Thomas Hart Benton (1889–1975) was an artist who painted images of everyday people in everyday life. He was born in Neosho and lived in Kansas City.

Chuck Berry (1926–) is a musician often called the father of rock and roll. Musicians such as Elvis Presley and the Rolling Stones admired and imitated him. He was born in Saint Louis.

George Washington Carver (1864?–1943) was a scientist at Tuskeegee Institute in Alabama. Carver (pictured above left) developed hundreds of new products from peanuts and other crops. He was born near Diamond Grove.

Walter Cronkite (1916–) was a widely respected news reporter on radio and television. He was born in Saint Joseph.

Thomas Stearns (T. S.) Eliot (1888–1965) was a poet. He won the 1948 Nobel Prize for literature. His *Old Possum's Book of Practical Cats* was made into the musical *Cats.* He was born in Saint Louis.

Langston Hughes (1902–1967) was an author who wrote poetry, novels, plays, short stories, and newspaper columns. He wrote about the African-American experience. He was born in Joplin.

John Huston (1906–1987) was a movie director. His movies include *The Maltese Falcon, Moby Dick,* and *The Man Who Would Be King.* He was born in Nevada, Missouri.

Jesse James (1847–1882) was an outlaw who robbed banks and trains. He was born in Kearney.

Scott Joplin (1868–1917) was a pianist and composer. He made ragtime music popular. Joplin was born in Texas and began his music career in Sedalia, Missouri.

Joseph Pulitzer (1847–1911) was a Saint Louis newspaper publisher. He set up the Pulitzer Prizes for writers and musicians.

Dred Scott (1795?–1858) was a slave who sued his master for freedom. He filed suit in the Saint Louis Circuit Court. He lost his case in the U.S. Supreme Court.

Harry Truman (1884–1972) was the thirty-third president of the United States (1945–1953). He was a U.S. senator from Missouri and served as vice president under President Franklin D. Roosevelt.

Mark Twain (1835–1910) was a well-loved writer. His favorite tales are *The Adventures of Tom Sawyer* and *The Adventures of Huckleberry Finn.* The real name of Mark Twain was Samuel Langhorne Clemens.

Laura Ingalls Wilder (1867–1957) wrote the Little House books. Born in Wisconsin, she moved to Mansfield, Missouri, in 1894. That's where she wrote her books.

Want to Know More?

At the Library

Doherty, Craig A. and Katherine M. *The Gateway Arch.* Woodbridge, Conn.: Blackbirch Press, 1995.

Welsbacher, Anne. *Missouri.* Edina, Minn.: Abdo & Daughters, 1998.

Wilder, Laura Ingalls. *On the Way Home: The Diary of a Trip from South Dakota to Mansfield, Missouri, in 1894.* New York: HarperTrophy, 1994.

Young, Judy, and Ross Young (illustrator). *S Is for Show Me: A Missouri Alphabet.* Chelsea, Mich.: Sleeping Bear Press, 2001.

On the Web

For more information on this topic, use FactHound.

1. Go to *www.facthound.com*
2. Type in this book ID: 0756503299
3. Click on the *Fetch It* button.

FactHound will find the best Web sites for you.

Through the Mail

Department of Economic Development
P.O. Box 1157
Jefferson City, MO 65102
For information on Missouri's economy

Missouri Division of Tourism

P.O. Box 1055
Jefferson City, MO 65102
For information on travel and interesting sights in Missouri

State Historical Society of Missouri

1020 Lowry
Columbia, MO 65201
For information about Missouri's history

On the Road

Mark Twain Boyhood Home and Museum
208 Hill Street
Hannibal, MO 63401
573/221-9010
To see where Mark Twain grew up

Missouri History Museum
5700 Lindell Boulevard
Saint Louis, MO 63112
314/746-4599
To explore Missouri's history

Missouri State Capitol
201 West Capitol Avenue
Jefferson City, MO 65101
573/751-4127
To visit the state capitol

Index

About the Author

Ann Heinrichs grew up in Fort Smith, Arkansas, and lives in Chicago. She is the author of more than eighty books for children and young adults on Asian, African, and U.S. history and culture. Ann has also written numerous newspaper, magazine, and encyclopedia articles. She is an award-winning martial artist, specializing in t'ai chi empty-hand and sword forms.

Ann has traveled widely throughout the United States, Africa, Asia, and the Middle East. In exploring each state for this series, she rediscovered the people, history, and resources that make this a great land, as well as the concerns we share with people around the world.